SHIFTING

YOUR MINDSET

A Guide to Overcome Depression, Anxiety and Trauma

Peace + Bliss,

Shawnee Palmer

SHAWNEE PALMER, LCSW, LAC

First Printing, 2020

ISBN 978-1-7355688-0-5

E-book ISBN: 978-1-7355688-1-2

Edited by: Chanteria Milner

Cover design by: Jacquitta McManus

Love & Serenity Wellness

PO Box 572

Chesterfield, MO 63006

www.loveandserenitywellness.com

Dedication

To my son Bryant, thank you for your patience and support. You've been a vital part of my healing journey!

Table of Contents

Preface

If you had a chance to redo your life, what would you change about it?

There have been many times in my life when I've felt a desire to go back in time and change the way I'd responded to a situation. For example, after my senior year of high school, I had an opportunity to relocate to another state. Instead, I decided to stay in my hometown for a relationship that I was afraid of letting go of. Six months later, I found myself full of regret. I felt stuck like I was missing out on freedom. The life that I'd envisioned with my then-partner wasn't playing out how I thought it would. However, I didn't want to confront these feelings. Instead, I stayed busy to get my mind off of things. I didn't want to feel that pain. I deserved a better life, and I didn't think that what I was experiencing was fair. But, instead of changing things, I drowned myself in work and school to help ease the pain. I admit, this helped during the day; however, when night came, everything started to rush back in, all of the sadness, tears, the thoughts racing through my head, trying to remind myself of the good times that I had in my relationship to distract myself from the present bad. With this, self-doubt started to creep in. I tried to make the situation better by focusing on money. I was overworking myself, but the money started to flow in. With this came health problems: high blood pressure, more anxiety, restless nights. I began to overreact to simple things that would have otherwise made me laugh or smile. I started to take things too seriously with the people around me. I felt like the world was against me and that no one could help me with my pain but me. I felt isolated and disconnected from everyone except for my son. My son is what helped me to keep going when I felt like I no longer wanted to move on.

This was the beginning of what I now recognize as depression. I would always think, what if I had made the decision to move? This thought replayed itself over and over again in my mind for years. I wanted a re-do. It wasn't until seven years later that I made the move out of state. I finally recognized that the goals that I had built up for myself could not be achieved by staying in my hometown. I wanted to leave behind the memories of my youth. I wanted to better myself for my then four-year-old son. He deserved more, and I knew that by moving, I would be able to give that to him.

That is where a new chapter of life started for me. Through the move, I found out why redoing my life wasn't the best thought to have. I recognized that, for most times in life, things don't happen the way we envision them. This is not because we failed, but because they weren't supposed to happen how we wanted them to. Had I moved to another state seven years earlier, my life may have been completely different, with challenges that I can't even imagine. I now look at my decision as a blessing in disguise.

I was only able to have this realization after I shifted my mindset.

Many times, we feel like life has slipped us by, leaving us in positions where we feel perpetually hopeless. We feel uncomfortable, anxious, and lost. Does this resonate with you? Do you ever feel like you want to give up?

Giving up would be the easiest thing to do. However, you have the ability to fight for what you want in life. Once you start fighting, you'll create an instinct within yourself that will make you stronger. Your fight will strengthen your mind, your views of yourself, and it will help you get more in tune with who you are and back on track toward your goals.

Are you ready for that? Are you prepared to fight?

I decided to write this book because I want to help guide other people out of their own mental war. I've battled with myself internally without much external discussion about it. From a very young age, I felt that my opinions and feelings didn't matter, so I only spoke about the positive aspects of me. Whenever I would express myself, I felt like I was being judged and looked down upon. But enough is enough.

This book was designed with you in mind, to help you overcome the challenges that have left you feeling stuck, confused, and low. In order to move toward living a better life for yourself, you have to develop positive ideas about your self-worth and your past choices. You have to heal from challenges and traumas that you have to face. After reading this book, you'll face all of these things. In the end, you will leave this book with a deeper understanding of who you are and the control that you have over your life.

Part 1

Attuning to Yourself

The first step on any path to radical change and discovery is to attune to yourself. This involves recognizing a self-care plan that is catered toward your specific needs, confronting your ideas about yourself, and learning how and when to pause and reflect on your own thoughts and actions. After this, you will have the tools needed to address your past challenges and traumas in a safe and healthy way.

Chapter 1

Self-care

Love yourself, cherish yourself, be kind and gentle with yourself, always.

Self-care is a commonly used term. However, many don't know what it should look like or how to apply it in their everyday lives. Creating a healthy self-care routine has been vital for me because it has allowed me to honor my internal needs. Everyone's self-care needs are unique to them; for me, I desire daily mental stimulation. I need to eat good food, express my thoughts through journaling, and connecting with my loved ones, and I need to feel at peace. Part of my self-care routine involves me writing in my journal every night to explore what the day looked like for me and the different emotions that I experienced. I also pray and take hot baths once a week to decompress. At least once a month, I eat at one of my favorite restaurants. On some Sundays, I go to a park to read a book while sitting in the grass, which allows me to ground myself and connect with nature.

All of these practices have been catered to my needs and have taken time and effort on my part to explore. You may not even recognize some of these practices as being part of a self-care routine. Everyone can sit in the grass; so, what?

But that's not the point. The point is that I have found practices that promote my own mental wellbeing and that allow me to hit reset on the different stressors in my life.

While I was in school, my professors spoke to us about preventing burnout in our work environments. I was able to balance work and home life easily because of this as I would make it a priority to leave work at work. However, this became an issue with one employer which made my work became very stressful. I eventually quit. I had to leave a job doing what I loved because I wasn't being treated fairly and my self-care needs were not being respected. Sometimes, this is what self-care looks like: leaving the things that you have worked hard toward because they are encroaching on your well-being. In that situation, self-care involved me taking the initiative to find a different job. By doing this, I was able to find a job that was less stressful and gave me extra financial freedom. I have also been able to devote more time to taking care of and connecting with my son.

Having an understanding of your own self-care needs is integral to your overall wellbeing. When someone lacks understanding of self-care, it often has a lot to do with their environment and the things that they have been exposed to. If you grew up in a home where an authority figure did not practice self-care, then it may be difficult for you to visualize it. However, everyone benefits when one engages in routine self-care, especially loved ones. If you are not taking care of yourself, how are you truly taking care of others?

If you are sick and bedridden, then how will the people you love and cherish benefit? The more you take care of yourself, the better the quality of effort you can put into everything that you do, which means that you can enhance the food that you cook, the emotional support that you provide, and the affection that you give to others. It'll all feel natural.

In order to start on this journey toward shifting your mindset and achieving your goals, you have to devote time to taking care of yourself. Many of the topics that will be covered in this book will be challenging. They will force you to reflect on traumatic events that you've had in your life, negative thoughts that you have about yourself and your environment, and unresolved challenges that you have let fester in the back of your mind. Each chapter will leave you exhausted, and it will feel like more harm than good is coming from them. These are the sacrifices needed for radical self-change. However, in order to get through it, you have to have a strong self-care foundation in order to ensure your mental and physical wellbeing.

So, what can self-care look like for you?

Speaking positively about yourself is self-care. Assessing the different stressors in your life and taking the time to consider if they are worth it is self-care. Taking time out of your day to engage in individual activities such as journaling, meditation, or prayer is self-care. Often people speak about how it's embarrassing, and it feels awkward for them to go out to dinner or the movies by themselves. Why do you feel that it would be awkward for you to be in your own company? Who taught you to feel embarrassed?

Everyone needs to practice self-care. You are not exempt.

Below are some activities that you can try in order to start your self-care journey. While there are hundreds of things that you can do to enjoy the company of yourself, these practices will also help you discover who you are. By engaging in solo activities, you gain insight towards things that you like or dislike about yourself, and they allow you to sit still with yourself in a non-judgmental space. Finally, when your life feels challenging, or you are faced with a difficult situation, having a self-care routine or self-care practices on hand will help you to take a breath, to reset, and to prepare yourself for the obstacle at hand.

Exercises:

Note: try to do these by yourself.

1. Check out the local listings for the next 30 days to see when you can plan a date and place to take yourself out.
2. Check out a new dinner spot at a restaurant that you have never eaten at before. Maybe try some new, fresh foods!
3. Get a journal or use the notes app in your phone to start jotting down the different challenges you face or emotions that you experience throughout the day.
4. Go to a shopping center where you can try on different clothes and accessories that make you feel good about yourself.
5. Try a new spa where you can get a facial, manicure-pedicure, or massage.

6. Go to a park and find a beautiful area where you can lay down a blanket and read a book, journal, or just listen to music.
7. Take a drive in an area where the scenery is peaceful and beautiful.
8. Try a new yoga or dance class.
9. Try a local winery where you can experience a wine tasting.
10. Research your local painting areas so you can try out painting or pottery.

Reflection:

Here are some questions that you can ask yourself. These will be especially helpful if you want to add journaling as a part of your self-care routine but don't know where to start.

Is there one activity that you are drawn to, but have not gotten around to doing it? Why is that? What is keeping you from that activity? Is there a way to navigate that situation?

How did you feel before doing one of these activities, during the planning stage?

While participating in the activity, be sure to make a mental note of how you feel during it. After, ask yourself: what were those feelings? Was that an activity that I would like to do again?

Did any negative feelings or experiences come up during that activity? Write those down, too.

Journal Your Thoughts & Feelings

Chapter 2

Self-esteem and Self-worth

All the money in the world will never add up to your true worth.

Your self-esteem is how you view your complete self, which means how you feel about your appearance, skills, career, finances, home life, and relationships with others. When you have low self-esteem, you tend to feel disconnected and uncertain about who you are. Sometimes, it can be as simple as disliking how you look or not trusting your ability to accomplish your life goals. Low self-esteem can infiltrate any area of our lives and cause us to lose touch with our true value and worth. Trust me, I know. I've struggled with my skin color and my weight throughout my entire life. Growing up, I was my mother's only brown-skinned child. This made me feel out of place like I didn't belong. In all of the pictures of our family, I stuck out. Even though I completely resemble my mother, I don't have her copper complexion, which made me feel like I wasn't pretty. My parents constantly told me how beautiful I was, but I didn't believe it for myself. It wasn't their validation that I was seeking, but my peers'.

On top of this, due to the different traumas that I'd experienced growing up, I ate to help ease the pain. Eating became a part of my life that soothed me. This overeating caused me to always carry more weight than my peers. Even though being overweight was the norm in my family, it wasn't something that I liked for myself.

I was able to overcome my negative feelings toward my skin color at a young age. Being in school and surrounded by others who were the same complexion as me helped to make me feel more at ease in my skin. However, I would still hide my body under baggy clothes, too afraid to wear things that fit snug. It felt like such an insurmountable challenge for me and completely eroded my self-esteem and the worth that I placed on myself. However, I was able to overcome this as well. I started to learn more about my body type. I took the steps toward getting healthy and losing weight. I bought clothes that I liked on my body instead of wearing ones that hid it. I started to feel more confident in myself.

I made the necessary changes both in my mindset and in my actions that helped me to build my self-esteem and affirm my self-worth.

Having low self-esteem can cause you to rely on other people for your own validation. It can make you short-change yourself in life, dissuade you from achieving your goals, and cause you to attract relationships and opportunities that you believe reflect the low value that you place on yourself. In this way, you will remain unchallenged, unenlightened, and dissatisfied with your life.

Everything that you do should add value to your life, not depreciate it.

At some point in our lives, we desire to make a change to ourselves. These can be any number of changes for any types of reasons; yet, before making any drastic changes, you have to overcome any negative thoughts that you have about yourself so that they do not continue to linger throughout your new life. Even when you make the physical change, the internal challenges don't magically go away. Learning to love both your new and old self requires you to enjoy the ugly parts that make you who you are. And guess what? Those ugly parts can only truly be defined by you and no one else unless you've internalized critiques from other people.

How do you create self-love? It's simple: you tackle the qualities that you feel are undesirable and turn them into something that soothes and enlightens your spirit when you think of them. This mental transformation is the power of alchemy, where you transform a negative into a positive. The way we react to our external word is based on our internal interpretation of life. These interpretations are our own; for example, if you believe that you will always feel happy when it is sunny outside, it will be so. In the same way, if you choose to label sitting in traffic as an unpleasant or irritating experience, it will also be so. With the power of alchemy, we recognize the power that we as individuals have over our thoughts and feelings. With it, you are able to take the negative feeling that you have about an aspect of yourself – whether that be your appearance, your job, or your home situation –and choose how you feel about it and react to it. Anyone can undergo this kind of mental transformation; the question is, how determined will you be to remain consistent with creating the new thought patterns? Let's get into exploring it more.

When participating in mental alchemy, there is a standard process that you should follow: Create >Practice> Feel> Share

First, you must *create* the new thought. If you believe that sitting in traffic is unpleasant, change this belief. Think about the positives that sitting in traffic give you: extra time to unwind and reflect by yourself; or, time to fit in other activities that you may not have time for in your busy schedule, such as listening to a podcast or audiobook.

Next, you must *practice* the thought. The next time you are in traffic, your first instinct will be to go back to your original belief about it. When this happens, you have to stop and remind yourself of the new thought that you've created.

Then, you must *feel* the thought. The longer that you practice targeting the negative thought when it comes and replacing it with the positive, the more you will begin to actually feel and believe in that new thought, until it becomes solidified in your mind. When that happens, you have successfully changed an unpleasant experience – in this case, sitting in traffic – into a positive.

Finally, try to *share* the thought. If you hear a close friend or family member complaining about traffic, try to suggest that they think about it the way that you do. The same applies to when you are changing a negative belief that you may have had about yourself. If you see someone close to you having similar negative thoughts about their appearance or life, offer them your now positive alternative.

Exercises:

Now that you have learned the mental transformation model, answer these questions about your own self-esteem and self-worth:

What are five negative thoughts that you have about yourself?

Why do you feel that these thoughts are real?

Would you like to change these thoughts?

Transform the thoughts below into five compliments that you've never given to yourself. Use either your name or "I" statements. For example, "Sherry, you are a great cook," or "I am a great cook":

1.
2.
3.
4.
5.

Now take some time to read these statements to yourself out loud. For additional help, ask someone close to you to read them aloud, using your name as they read.

Tip: Record yourself on your phone reading them, then play it back to hear your voice. Play this recording as often as you need when you are feeling lonely, a lack of support, or unwanted.

Reflection:

What emotions or thoughts came to mind while doing this exercise? Think about the five thoughts that you changed; are these thoughts that you would like to keep? If not, how would you like to feel?

Think about your own self-value. Is there something that you would like to value more within yourself? Often, we value family, traditions, humor, hobbies, or titles. Do you value yourself enough to choose yourself over another individual who makes you sad or overly emotional? How do you handle constructive criticism? If someone is providing you with a suggestion on what you should change about yourself, are you more motivated to make that change than if it was self-motivated?

If you valued yourself a little more, how do you think you'd feel? How do you think people would perceive you? Would it change your relationships with some people? Would these individuals no longer want to engage with you? If they wouldn't, take some time to reflect on how that would affect you. Would it make you feel less of a decent person?

If the way individuals perceive you dictates how you value yourself, then it's time to consider those friendships or relationships that you have.

If it feels right for you to value yourself more, there should be no thought into how others view you. The way that you feel about yourself should be exclusive to you alone. If you start to do something to improve yourself and others are bothered by it, then how necessary is it that you continue having them in your life? If you start to notice this, then that is confirmation that you are on the right path. Many will follow your lead while others fall behind! This is part of the life cycle; are you ready for this to happen? Though it will be challenging, you must prepare for this reality. If you desire better in life, then things in your environment must change in some manner.

Remember to follow the model: Create> Practice> Feel It> Share. This complete exercise is how you replace and release unwanted thoughts and feelings through your actions for yourself and others.

Finally, if you find yourself in an unhealthy mindset after going through any of the topics discussed, whether that be because of unearthed feelings or any other cause, be sure to head back to chapter one and practice one or more of the self-care activities that you have generated for yourself.

Journal Your Thoughts & Feelings

Chapter 3

Trusting Yourself

Intuition was a gift given to you at birth. Use it to the best of your ability. Make it work for you.

Learning to trust myself was one of the hardest things for me to do. I never used to rely on my own intuition; I was too afraid of failure and of things going wrong. This fear was caused by my own self-doubt, which clouded my judgment and caused me more internal chaos than necessary. I did this when making any types of decisions: about which college classes to take, places to live, people to talk to, or jobs to take. Sometimes it could be as small as getting a gut feeling to take a different route while driving in order to avoid heavy traffic that I don't listen to. In return, this caused me repeated irritation and distrust within myself over time to the point that I just didn't understand myself. For some reason, I just couldn't get it right, and I felt that I should've listened to myself. This was especially hard for me when it came to the relationships that I had growing up. I expected people to have my best interest at heart. I am passionate about being honest and good to others, so I felt that they would feel the same toward me. In my relationships, I would ignore red flags in others' behaviors because I didn't trust myself to make the decision to take someone out of my life. What if they could be better? What if I just wasn't giving them a chance? I refused to listen to my intuition in exchange for these "what if" situations.

Growing up, I learned time after time that people can hurt you. However, I was taught that no matter how much someone hurt you, it is okay for them to remain in your life. My intuition would tell me to let go of a friendship or relationship, however, I wouldn't do so because I was listening to these childhood lessons and I was fearful of the backlash that might come with me letting people go. I knew it was best for me, but I was fearful of how it would impact the other person. I cared more about their feelings than my own. I knew that I was limiting myself when fear became my best friend. Fear was taking over my life. It held me back from exploring the unknown, the unlimited possibilities of everything--my career, relationships, and education.

As a result, I became a master at limiting myself. I battled with this for several years until I learned to let that fear go and begin trusting myself.

How often do you spend time battling with your thoughts? Do you find yourself doing this frequently? Why do you do it?

Intuition

We often hear from others about how important it is to trust your intuition, but how do you know if it's your intuition or someone else's thoughts or opinions? When it comes from within, there should be no questioning it. Your first thought is most likely the answer you've been seeking. You may feel like the thought came to you because you have been feeling obsessive over something, but why do you think that obsession is there? Was your initial thought reasonable, or did it sound delusional? If it feels delusional, you may be obsessing over the topic. If that's the case, it's time for you to clean out your home.

Exercise:

Clutter of any kind typically starts within the mind. When we have over-cluttered the brain, we tend to transfer it into our physical spaces i.e.: cars and homes. The brain has the capacity to only hold so much stress until it disperses into the body. Our homes represent who we are internally and every inch of it holds our energy within it. Whatever your eyes latch onto in any environment can impact you. If you can sit in your home, which is supposed to be the most peaceful space, you can take in the energy that was left in the home. If it's unclean and has old items and energy in it, you will continue to absorb it. To clear out the clutter in your brain, you need to feel renewed and fresh. When you clean physically, it causes some of the mental stress that you've built up to be released. Your mind needs a fresh view of your home.

You will be able to trust your intuition when distractions are removed. The clutter or oldness in the home represents your brain. Clearer thoughts increase your ability to listen to your intuition. There will be less doubt and more concentration.

31

Creating time to clean your home.

The mind picks up on visuals, and the chaos in your home can trigger more disorder mentally. Your thoughts can begin to feel overwhelming, unmanageable, and out of control. To get your mind back in line, you can shift things backward, meaning that you can work on clearing out your home and then work on the clutter within your brain. Focus on cleaning spaces that you spend a lot of time in. These areas need to be clear so that you have room to breathe. By being clean, they will bring you visual stability when you look at them daily.

Set aside some time, starting with 10-15 minutes a day for the next seven days, to clean one area of your home. If writing your plan down on paper gives you a better visual, then it is highly recommended that you do so. Take some time and walk around your home before you start to clean and take inventory of what you feel needs to change. Choose seven different tasks that you'd like to set for yourself. Next, choose which day you'll do what. After you've established that plan, take one day to prepare to do so mentally. Sit in a quiet space for 5-10 minutes and close your eyes, then start to visualize yourself doing the activities of day one. If you're feeling up to it, go through the next six days during that same sitting. If it's difficult for you to do all seven days in one session, focus on visualizing yourself doing one task each day before the actual job itself.

Journal Your Thoughts & Feelings

_____
_____
_____
_____
_____
_____
_____
_____
_____
_____
_____
_____
_____
_____
_____
_____
_____
_____
_____
_____
_____
_____
_____
_____
_____
_____
_____
_____

Chapter 4

Self-criticism

*Judging yourself can create barriers that feel
insurmountable. Quit seeking out imperfections and
focus on your strengths.*

Why do people criticize themselves? It can often come from familial or societal expectations that were drilled into you as a child. Growing up, I was told that my opinions didn't matter. When I was vocal about how different things made me feel, I was dismissed. As a result of this, I criticized myself as a teenager and an adult for having the desire to speak my true feelings to others. I didn't feel that it was my place. Even when I went to school, I didn't participate outside of my academics; I didn't know that I could speak my opposing views and be heard. I had learned to dismiss my own thoughts. I overly criticized myself based on beliefs instilled in me as a child, which caused me to suffer in silence and accept other's thoughts and feelings more than my own as an adult. In this way, my self-criticism was a brutal response toward myself that limited the way that I could communicate with the world.

On the other hand, self-criticism can also be a positive thing. Self-criticism should help you improve upon yourself. It should reveal qualities about yourself and motivate you to grow into a more enjoyable, healthy version of yourself. It should not make you hide aspects of yourself or make you less able to speak for yourself, as had happened in my life. Yet, this kind of positive criticism often comes with abandoning harmful beliefs that you were given as a child. It requires an alternative approach to how you look at yourself and your role in the world.

Ask yourself: Is it easy for you to identify things about yourself that you'd like to change or improve? Are these ideas self-driven, or are they created based on what other people have said about you?

Many people can look in the mirror and find physical things that they strongly dislike about themselves. They can have on their favorite outfit and still focus on a blemish or extra stomach fat that they see as displeasing. These people find things about themselves that they don't like and open themselves up to negative self-talk about their appearance. This creates an unhealthy way of looking at yourself. Are you one of these people? Do you often focus on traits that you don't like about yourself, and tear yourself apart about them in an unhealthy way?

What about all of those times you may have done something well, and when people praised you for it, you dismissed it and responded by saying, "Oh, I could've done better." When you think back on all of the times that you've criticized yourself, view the patterns, and identify what specifically is the number one thing you criticize yourself about. It's easy to get wrapped up in comparing yourself to what others feel you should be, but it's another thing to be unconscious of how often you critique yourself due to society's views. The conversation that you have with yourself is the most important. Identify each situation in which you do this and where it stems from.

Throughout my lifetime, I've felt that I wouldn't succeed in my goals. I was a perfectionist, and if I didn't perform at my best in relationships, school, or work, I felt bad about myself. I wanted everyone to see the greatness within me. As I've grown older, I look back and recognize that I didn't see the greatness in myself, so it was impossible for others to do the same.

Being able to critique things about yourself will possibly be easy. People are usually their own worst critics. However, they can also be their biggest cheerleaders. People often seek these validating moments from others, but what if you were able to create it for yourself? This would be beneficial because it would allow you to create validation in a way that would be most helpful and realistic for you. Overall this would give you an abundance of confidence and lay a solid foundation for building self-actualization, where you fully realize your potential.

Exercise:

Answer the following questions:

1. What are some (non-physical) things that you adore about yourself (your sense of humor, your aspirations, etc.)?

2. What are some physical features that you like about yourself?

3. What do you see as some of your strengths?

4. How have these characteristics benefited you throughout your lifetime?

5. Was there ever a time that these characteristics were a disadvantage for you? If so, how?

6. Are there any aspects of yourself that you would like to change? Why? Figuring out the root causes of the displeasure that you have in yourself will help you determine whether or not you are exhibiting positive or negative self-criticism.

Journal Your Thoughts & Feelings

Chapter 5

Self-discovery through Self-love

What you see behind your eyes is what leads you to your desired destination.

As I moved through life, I often felt lost, confused, and misunderstood. Growing up, I'd always felt out of place: either I spoke too proper or I was too smart compared to those around me. I didn't struggle in school; it was natural for me to learn quickly and perform well on my assignments. I was always on the honor roll and received praise for my educational efforts and accomplishments. Throughout my childhood and through college, I continued learning and overachieving all of my expectations. Although I grew up in a family that didn't attend college or place pressure on me to do so, when I went, I still felt that it was my job to show my family that there was another way of living life. My family worked typical 9-5 jobs, overworking themselves, and barely making ends meet. I observed how they were living all my life. During these observations, I would make a mental note to do better in my future. I felt that it was my responsibility to do better. Still, I didn't understand that, for me to do that, I needed to go through a series of challenges to help shape me into who I truly needed to be to succeed and break free from the norms, values, and morals of my childhood life.

Yet, throughout everything, my schoolwork provided me with the validation that I needed. I became comfortable with my identity after hearing from professors, colleagues, and peers glorify my intellectual gifts. I knew that there was a higher calling for my life and that I had to stay on track so that I could refine my goals and gain a better understanding of my life purpose.

Throughout life, you will have many moments of self-discovery. As you reflect on your life, would you say that you are satisfied with who you are? Do you lack knowledge and understanding of who you are? Clearing your thoughts and learning about the things that bring you joy, pain, and fear will help you to have a better understanding of why you operate the way that you do in life. Discovering yourself can help you analyze and prioritize your life. I strived to achieve higher education and focus on my learning as a result of the struggles I witnessed my parents and family members face. What are the core motivations for the things that you do?

In all, this process of self-discovery cannot happen without internalizing the different lessons that you have learned so far in this book, namely your self-care routine, recognizing your self-worth, and most importantly, developing your self-love. I often felt embarrassed whenever my family members would point out my love for reading and learning, or the way I spoke, or the activities that I participated in; it was not until I embraced these characteristics as core aspects of my identity did I recognize my path and therefore discover myself and my life goals.

Exercises:

First, let us focus on developing self-love. This is a foundational step toward self-discovery; only through accepting yourself the way that you are will you be able to recognize your true dreams and goals, rather than those that you have convinced yourself are true.

Consider this: what does it mean to love yourself?

For me, loving myself means taking a step back when I am experiencing challenges and participating in self-care activities. It means recognizing when I am in the wrong in a situation and carefully showing myself what's right. It means constant but careful self-criticism to ensure that I am on the best path possible toward promoting my own happiness and achieving what I want from life. Now ask yourself:

> How does it make you feel to think about loving yourself more than you do now? You may not even recognize seeds of self-hatred that may have been implanted in you over your life. What do you see as the least loveable aspect of yourself? Why do you think that is?

> How do you practice self-love right now? *Do* you practice self-love? How would you like to practice self-love?

> What do you need to help you with self-love? It's completely fine to accept outside help to promote your own self-love at the beginning. For me, that outside help came in the form of validation from my teachers and peers. Now, I am able to generate my own self-love, something I would not have been able to do had I not had that help in the beginning.

43

In order to begin practicing self-love, do the following activity daily. Doing this activity daily will help build a self-love routine for you, which will eventually normalize the idea of self-love and lead you to explore personal ways of loving yourself.

Find a comfortable, quiet space to do this activity. You can do this with your eyes open or closed. Take a few deep breaths in and out before starting.

State the following affirmation: "I am open to receiving the love, peace, and happiness that surrounds me."

Recite this affirmation three times, then visualize yourself letting go of any emotional disturbance that you may be feeling. Focus on releasing the old so that you can accept the new that is coming into your life.

Repeat this exercise as often as you need until you feel a sense of comfort. This exercise can be done daily for a specific time frame. For example, you can do this for a week straight or kick it up a notch and do it for 21 days as a self-healing ritual.

Doing these exercises in combination with the other self-care activities that you have been participating in before starting the next chapters will be beneficial if you have a lot of unresolved issues from past traumas or life experiences, as the rest of this book will work toward rooting those issues out.

Now that you have recognized ways to promote your own self-love, let's look at moving toward self-discovery.

For many people, they can divide their life into chapters. This can be done based on schooling (i.e. a pre-school chapter, an elementary school chapter, and so on up until you have finished school); it can be based on the different life phases you have gone through (childhood, adolescence, young-adulthood, etc.); it can be based on influential events that happened throughout your life; or it can just be a simple feeling that you get when you think about different parts of your life. Choose one of these methods to divide your life up. Now, think about the person that you were during each of the different chapters, and ask yourself these questions:

What were 2-3 main characteristics of yourself during that time. Were you an avid reader? Were you active? Did you care about social issues? Were you more outgoing, or did you like to spend more time by yourself during?

What were a few of the goals that you had during each of the chapters? If you didn't have any, especially when thinking about childhood, that fine! Just answer this question for as many of the chapters that you can.

Who were the most influential people on your life during each of these chapters? What is one way that person influenced you?

Are there any characteristics, goals, or people that have been consistent throughout most or all of the chapters of your life? If so, these are the beginnings of your core identity. Recognizing the different aspects of your core identity will aid you on your path towards establishing or clarifying your life goals and the steps needed to help you reach those goals.

Now that you have reflected on your past, think about the present. What are 3 things that you care about the most? This can be a person or people, a social issue, an activity, whatever is important to you now.

> Consider how those things affect the decision that you make on a day-to-day basis; do the things that you care about guide the choices that you make every day? How do they influence the activities that you participate in today, including your job? If they don't, reflect on why that is, and the different changes that you could make to increase the impact that these things have on your life.

Finally, let's look toward the future.

> What are 3 short term (one to six months) goals that you have? How are you working toward those goals? What keeps you motivated toward achieving those goals?

> Is there something that you have always fantasized about doing, such as writing a book, going on a trip, or learning a language? Are you working toward these dreams in any way?

Answering these questions about your past and present realities, as well as your future goals, will not only better clarify the kind of person that you are and the things that you care about, but it will also help you begin to recognize the different motivators in your life, which will help you become more likely to achieve your goals.

Only through self-love and then self-discovery will you be able to achieve the wonderful things that you want to do in your life. I am a testament to this; only through growing to love the identity that was contrary to my family, recognizing how that identity influenced my goals, and acknowledging the different motivators in my life was I able to eventually achieve my goals of a higher education, which has led me to live the life that I love today.

Journal Your Thoughts & Feelings

Chapter 6

Managing Your Fear and Anxiety

Anxious thoughts come and go. Don't let them get the best of you.

Anxiety is the cause of an event or idea that excessively replays in your mind. It can happen when you feel overwhelmed, or when you have developed excessive fear toward experiencing something. This anxiety becomes so big that you can no longer concentrate on other things or control your thoughts. Sometimes, it can manifest physically, such as feeling choked up. You may have a racing heartbeat, changes in your breathing, or feel shakiness in your hands, arms, or legs. You may also notice a difference in your body temperature or begin to feel faint.

Does this ever happen to you?

There are different types of anxiety. For example, social anxiety can happen as a result of being in large or public areas. Your body can tense up in these settings, and you can start to feel suffocated and trapped. It makes you feel as if you are unable to articulate your ideas or be your authentic self. It makes you want to run and hide. People who suffer from social anxiety appear to be awkward or standoffish when, in reality, they are just terrified! They're terrified that they will say the wrong thing, or they feel that others are looking at them as if they are weird or judging them.

Any feeling of anxiety can be uncomfortable and make you feel abnormal. Have you ever stood in front of a classroom to give a speech but couldn't find the right words to say? Or had a tough time pronouncing words that you typically know well? What about your first day on the job or interviewing for a job? It's not a very good feeling, but it is something that happens a lot. From childhood to adulthood, this is something that many people experience at every stage of their lives.

What all of these examples share is the root cause of fear.

At the age of 12, I learned that my uncle had gotten into a car accident. After he spent a few days in a coma at the hospital, he passed away. Although I didn't drive until I was 16, whenever I got in a car, I thought about the details of his car accident and had intense fear about it possibly happening to another loved one or myself. I felt this way until I became a driver myself. Even though it wasn't as intense as the first year after his death, when I began driving, I was on edge and very aware of the road, other drivers, and was obsessive about wearing a seat belt with each car ride I had.

It wasn't until I made the conscious decision to confront this fear did I begin to overcome my anxiety. Whenever I got behind the wheel and began feeling anxious, I would remind myself of all the times in which I haven't gotten into a car accident. I reminded myself that it was necessary for me to drive in order to take care of my needs. I did both of these practices while also playing calming, classical music in the car to keep the feelings at bay and remain focused. Eventually, I stopped thinking about the car accident whenever I got in the car, and I finally shed my fear of driving.

Think back to the last time that you felt anxious. What kind of setting were you in and what were you doing? What did that feel like for you? Did it become harder to breathe? Was this a random occurrence, or do you often feel anxious when you are in that situation?

Answering these initial questions will help identify the root fears that cause you to feel anxious and confront the cause of those anxious feelings.

The question that you may have now is, how do I get rid of this feeling when it hits me suddenly? Here are a few exercises to get you started.

Exercises:

For every feeling of anxiety, there is a trigger that causes it. When you experience stress, you typically allow it to build up before you take action to release it. It's common that you will let the thoughts fester until you feel on edge and experience physical discomfort. Now, why is this the first thing that you'd do? It has to do with the attention that you give it. The more focus and energy you place into a thought, the more likely the idea will grow. If you're able to dismiss or replace the thought, you'll find more success in preventing an anxious episode.

Dismissing a thought

Dismissing a thought can be done in many different ways. Have you ever heard someone say something to you that you knew wasn't right, so you stopped listening to them while they were still speaking? Or, have you ever known someone to speak ill of a situation, person, or thing and therefore decided that you don't want a part in their thinking? Well, the way that you've responded to others is the same way that you can respond to yourself when an anxious thought pop into your mind. You may tell yourself, "Today, I chose not to deal with this" or "I am not allowing this to bother me." These are just some statements to trigger your brain to shift gears. By doing this, you will not feed into the thought or allow it to grow.

Replacing a thought

Have you ever had a favorite shirt that you just could not stop wearing? You wore it so much that it started to look dingy, and now it has a few holes in it? Thoughts can be just like a favorite shirt that you wear too much. Sometimes you may use an idea over and over again because you've found comfort within the thought, consciously or unconsciously. Eventually, your brain will give you a signal that it's rejecting a thought, which results in the mind sending a message to the body that it's overwhelmed. When this happens, it means that the thought no longer gives you the satisfaction that it once potentially gave you. So just like old shirts, you have to eventually get new shirts to make you feel better, so you stop wearing the old one or throw it away.

Thoughts work the same way! If you tell yourself, "I am never going to pass this test," but you take the test and pass it, you may repeat this same statement each time you have a test, which can cause you to feel anxious about it. Imagine telling yourself three new thoughts to give you a more desirable feeling after using the statements. Instead of telling yourself you'll never pass the test, tell yourself, "I have always passed these tests in the past. I am confident that I can pass this test. I have studied long and hard, so I know most of the information." Now that was three new statements to overpower the one, worn down statement that no longer worked for you. This is the same process that I had to undertake when getting over my hear of driving: by replacing one negative thought with multiple positive affirmations.

Reflection:

Write five negative thoughts that you've had throughout your lifetime:

1.
2.
3.
4.
5.

Write five positive thoughts that you've had throughout your lifetime:

1.

2.

3.

4.

5.

Journal Your Thoughts & Feelings

Chapter 7

Managing Your Anger and Depression

*I was once in a dark place. Now, I've found
my way to the light.*

Managing Depression:

Depression looks different for everyone; however, one thing that remains constant is that it's uncomfortable and makes life complicated.

Have you ever experienced a low mood where you were tearful, and crying seemed to be the only option for relieving the pain that you felt? Have you ever felt sluggish with little to no motivation to do anything? What about little or no interest in socializing with others? Do your usual activities now seem like a task or chore? These are signs that you may be battling with depression.

Depression can cause you to lose sight of where you desire to be in life. It can also cause you to harbor old situations that happened years prior. It can feel like sudden sadness creeping up or lingering around you, poisoning everything that you do in your day-to-day life. To get through depression, you have to understand where it's rooted and find a routine of simple tasks that you can do to push through the discomfort.

What can you do while experiencing depression?

Identify whether or not you feel safe being alone. If you do not feel safe, find a safe environment that you can go to with people who you trust. Being in a secure environment can help lessen your symptoms.

You can provide comfort for yourself by using your senses. Everything that we do requires us to use one of them. Identifying different activities that you can do to alleviate your depression symptoms becomes easier when you focus on one sense at a time. To add, using your senses will help to ground you in the moment, which will draw you out of yourself and your feelings of depression. Let's take a closer look at what that should look like:

A. **Smell**: Find something that has a pleasant, soft aroma to it. Once you smell scents such as lavender or vanilla, a signal is sent to your brain that will provide you with comfort. These natural substances have chemical compounds that, when absorbed through any sense, gives a natural release of built-up sadness or stress. This activity can best be achieved by smelling essential oils or, if you have access to one, using a diffusor.

B. **Taste**: Allow yourself to have a small portion of something healthy and naturally sweet, such as fruit. This will allow you to gain and maintain energy in a healthy manner. You'd want to avoid sugary and unhealthy processed foods that cause a high followed by a quick low, such as coffee and sugar when experiencing depressive episodes.

C. **Touch**: If you have a pet or any soft fabric like silk, touch it, focusing on how it feels against your hands. This activity works well with water also.

D. **Sight**: As we discussed in the chapter about trusting yourself, your surroundings play a significant role in your mood. When you look around your environment, do you feel a sense of security? Does your space have any representation of who you are? If not, it may be time to redecorate and adorn the space with things that you like. For example, surround yourself with pictures of your favorite people or places you have traveled to or would like to go to. Also, having your favorite color or colors around helps to brighten the space.

E. **Sound**: Our bodies consist of unseen energy. All sound, such as music, emits a frequency that can shift energies to a high and low state. Have you ever been in a happy mood, but a sad song came onto the radio, and it made you feel down? Or what about a song that made you want to jump up and dance? The song may have had high energy levels in the melody, or the voice of the artist indicated that they had high energy levels when recording the song. I if you intentionally listen to music or sounds that calm the mind and body, you'll be able to raise your mood.

Sense-specific exercises such as these should be used in conjunction with the self-care regimens that you have developed for yourself in order to effectively prevent or lessen the effects of depressive episodes.

Exercise:

What can you do to prevent a deep depressive episode? Identify three things that you can do in the future:

1.

2.

3.

Expressing Anger:

Anger is a strong emotion that can be triggered by sadness, hurt, or hate. Anger can therefore derive from depression. Think about every single time you've experienced anger; more than likely, your anger was driven by expectations, an expectation that people would respect and honor things in the same manner in which you would do. When you have expectations about a person or situation, and it results in disappointment, it can be hard to cope with. Within a split second, you may feel rage. Some people may respond with tears, fear, or vulgar language. To add, anger can come suddenly or after anxious thoughts have built up. In this case, it's always best to take a step back and allow your emotions to flow through you rather than responding. Anger is a natural emotion, so it will not always be avoidable. Your values and beliefs about life contribute to how passionate you are about things that can trigger anger.

The reality is that people can be so self-centered and self-absorbed in their chaos that they don't recognize how their actions can cause a ripple effect on others. The best way to manage anger is to take anger and make it your best friend. Honor your anger by allowing it to be. Nurture it by validating why it's there. Coddle it with love rather than abandoning it by releasing it onto others. Your anger is unique to only you at that moment. You need to take control over it before it controls you and before you respond in ways that are out of character for you.

You can acknowledge that your anger is your own and teach yourself to respond to it differently. What does it look like to take ownership of your anger? There's not one way to do it because it should be tailored toward your personality and uniqueness.

Exercise:

Respond to anger in the following manner:

1. Sit
2. Think
3. Meditate
4. Speak

Sit: Find a comfortable, quiet space to sit in. Often, anger is accompanied by your heart racing, which causes you to take many shallow breaths. Focus on releasing bodily tension by controlling your breathing.

Think: Allow yourself to drift into a conversation with yourself to gain an understanding of why you feel angry. What happened leading up to you feeling angry? Was there a specific object of your anger (such as another person), or was it more general? Were you angry at something you did? Is your anger directed toward something that you can control?

Meditate: As you focus on your breathing, try to consider the different variables that contributed to your anger. To begin your meditation, release all of your anger mentally. Do this by imagining up the object of your anger and think about all of the things that they did, and the things that you did or wanted to say in response. This will work as a cathartic exercise, the same way that writing up an angry letter and then throwing it away would work. After you have exhausted what you wanted to say, pretend that you are breathing out all of the now consolidated anger until nothing remains.

Speak: Once you have finished meditating, it's time to confront the person or thing that caused your anger. If it was a person, use "I don't like it," or "I feel this way..." statements to begin the conversation and take time out to talk to the person that triggered the anger in a calm tone. We will go more in-depth into engaging with others in the next chapter.

Reflection:

These are the steps to follow for responding to depression:

1. Identify the change in mood and the trigger that caused it.
2. Seek safety.
3. Engage in a healthy coping skill.
4. Reflect on the episode so that you have a better understanding of it once you no longer have intense emotions about it. Reflect can take a few minutes or a few days to start.

Reflect on past depressive episodes that you've had. Identify as many details as you can about the experience while in a non-depressive state or, if you experience depression frequently, do this reflection during a time when you with a loved one or engaging in an activity, such as music, that eases some of your symptoms. What activities were you engaging in before the depressive episode happened? Were you around anyone and, if so, who? How long did the episode last? Were there any tasks that made you feel better or worse during the episode? How did you feel once the episode ended?

Taking the time to research and gain a better understanding of how your depressive episodes are caused and the root of where it derives from is essential. The moment that you become triggered is the moment where you should apply your intervention skills to increase comfort. Remember, you are to clear out the emotion from the trigger before responding to it. Seek support and safety before anything else.

Journal Your Thoughts & Feelings

Chapter 8

Communicating Your Thoughts and Feelings to Others

My thoughts are clear and concise. My feelings are valid.
I speak freely, and it makes me feel at peace.

Many people feel that they cannot be free and authentic with how they communicate their feelings towards others. This lack of communication causes you to withhold your genuine emotions, which can create undesirable interactions with others. Speaking your truth is a necessity when it comes to communication; how else are your needs going to be met by others if you don't first learn how to verbalize those needs? Understanding why you hold your thoughts and feelings back is a vital step toward developing effective communication skills and, as a result, being heard by others.

Many barriers cause communication breakdowns. Some people who are shy or quiet keep thoughts to themselves. Why does this happen? It can be due to fear of judgment from others, a desire to avoid rejection, the belief that their thoughts don't matter, or it could be that a person feels that others won't validate their voice. Whatever the cause, there is never a good reason to allow ideas to race in your mind without releasing them in some manner.

Why are you so silent? Why do you feel that your voice isn't necessary? Why do you sit and not respond to others when they make you feel uncomfortable? Your body is responding because you must answer. Your voice is connected to your body, and when they aren't aligned, they will operate from a place of chaos. Your body is begging you to release those thoughts so that it can stop taking on the burdens for your voice. Would you prefer harmony or confusion?

After reflecting on why you don't vocalize your thoughts, the next step is to advocate and communicate your feelings to others. You're doing great work, and all of the knowledge that you gain about yourself will help you to remove built-up stress. Telling others how you truly feel is essential as it shows them how they should proceed when responding to. Some individuals are accustomed to pressuring others to view things from their perspective; by learning to communicate effectively, it shows others that you will not accept this type of behavior.

I learned as a child that I wasn't supposed to talk back to my elders. To my family, advocating for myself and vocalizing my opinion about things would be considered talking back, which would lead to criticism or punishment. I also saw how other children in my family were treated if they did talk back. I wanted to avoid getting into trouble, so I kept thoughts to myself. I also learned during my childhood that even if I did speak up, my words were dismissed. I also had a lot of fear that I would be judged or looked down on because many of my thoughts and beliefs were different from around me. Because of this, I became a people pleaser, going along with things as I grew older to appease others. This impaired many of my personal and professional relationships throughout my life, where I struggled with feeling unheard and unimportant to the people that I was engaging with on the one hand but felt fearful that others would abandon or judge me if I vocalized my thoughts on the other.

I overcame this struggle by recognizing that my voice is valuable. In the work environment, I would get praise and acknowledgment of things that I spoke about. I started to grow great confidence due to this. I recognized how necessary communication was in friendships, family relationships, and intimate relationships. I started to just *speak*.

Exercise:

Typically, when people do not voice their opinions, they struggle with self-doubt and have low confidence in their voices being heard. These emotions come with a strong fear of judgment. People who are more confident understand the value of speaking up for themselves. Confidence allows you to speak about easy or difficult topics.

Reflect on a significant time in your life when you failed to express your genuine opinion due to your fear of how the other person would feel.

What were your initial thoughts regarding the situation?

Where and how often did you think about this situation after it occurred

When did you finalize your opinion about the situation? Did your thoughts change from your first reaction?

What was going on in your life at the time? Were you in a distressed or happy state? How could this have affected your response?

How was the information communicated to you? In what tone?

Focus on how you wanted to respond. Did you have a strong understanding of your emotions and thoughts during that time? Do you feel that you have a better understanding of your emotions now?

Here are some statements that you can use to begin formulating your own opinions. These will be especially helpful when you are expressing an opinion that may be contrary to the person that you are speaking with.

"I understand that this you believe this, and/but I feel ..."

"When you do [insert], it makes me feel [insert emotion]. This is what will make me feel more comfortable."

"I respect your opinion. However. . ."

Journal Your Thoughts & Feelings

Part 2

Looking to the Past

*Now that you have gained the tools and techniques needed
to better understand your present self, it is time to shift
scope. We must now look at the past, recognizing those
experiences that are still having a negative effect on us
today. Through this, you will have to confront challenging
and, for some, traumatic moments that happened in your
past. However, by confronting these experiences, you will
be able to understand how you may be replicating the
bad habits or experiences that you witnessed in your past,
which will better aid you on your process toward positive
self-discovery and change.*

Chapter 9

Traumatic Moments in Childhood & Adolescence

You have the power to control how your past experiences
affect your present reality.

From a young age, I was exposed to domestic violence and verbal abuse. I witnessed countless fights between family members and their partners. Often, when one of my family members didn't like someone else, they would resort to fighting them, even if that other person was also a member of the family. The police constantly visited my home due to these fights, so much so that I now cannot separate the memories of seeing police cars and seeing a family member beaten. Closer to home, my mother participated in this kind of domestic abuse. There was a time when I watched my mother stab her partner with a kitchen knife. The image would not leave my head for years. However, this behavior became normalized for me as my mother stayed with this partner, despite their frequent violence.

This kind of behavior filtered into my adult life. During my 20s, there were a few occasions where I opted to use violence out of anger with a partner. I acted directly as a result of what I'd learned in my childhood. However, those kinds of responses were out of character for me; realizing this helped me to become more aware of my actions and the toxicity of the relationship that I was in. I learned how important it was for me to end that relationship and instead focus on my own healing as I learned to manage my anger and confront my past traumas.

During your own childhood, you may have experienced traumas that left you feeling sad, uncertain, and confused on how to operate as an adult. You have to develop a better understanding of the things that have happened to you during your childhood in order to heal from those events. Now is the time to address those traumas in order to help rectify any problematic behaviors that you engage in today and to elevate your life further.

Are there any moments from your own childhood or adolescence that stand out to you as particularly concerning? Are there any habits or thought patterns that you participate in today that may be potentially harmful? Where do you think those came from?

One of the biggest influences during our childhoods and adolescence are the authority figures in our home. Not only do they guide our development, but they shape the behaviors and attitudes that we have toward life and other people. Additionally, these figures dictate how you are which affects different parts of your identity and your actions as an adult, such as your ideas surrounding justice and the way you may rear your own children.

In my own home, my mother was the prime authority figure. Even so, I was the one who primarily cared for my siblings. This caused me to mature faster than my peers, making me miss out on being a kid. My mother had high expectations of me and of my potential to care for my siblings; as a result, my mother primarily relied on verbal abuse as a way to discipline me. She would say harsh things about me, making me feel unworthy to myself. Her words lowered my self-esteem, but what hurt the most was hearing them come from someone who was supposed to love me the most. If my mother thought this way about me, then what could I have expected from a potential partner? Her discipline style as well as the way she coped with anger caused me, as an adult, to choose partners who spoke to me the same way and surround myself with people who replicated the abuse that my mother had attached to me. It wasn't until I recognized this patter that I was eventually able to change and take control over my life and the people I surrounded myself with.

Who was the authority figure in your house? When you made a mistake as a child and/or as a teenager, how did your parent(s) or guardian(s) react? Did they yell at you, or were they patient with you? Did they explain why they were angry? Did you begin to identify making mistakes as being a negative thing due to the way they responded?

How did it make you feel as a child knowing that you did not understand what you did wrong and why the authority figure in your house responded the way that they did? Do you catch yourself making mistakes and being angry with yourself the same way that a parent or guardian used to be with you? The trauma that we face as children and teenagers—including the way an authority figure disciplines us and the different experiences that we were subjected to—can cause us to develop harmful habits that permeate our present selves. The way you think about mistakes is one of these habits. In response to my own trauma and the troubling ideas that I had about myself, I began using alcohol to cope with life stressors. I neglected my own personal needs, became fearful of expressing my emotions, and began ostracizing the people who cared about me the most.

Many people respond differently to childhood trauma. Therefore, the habits that people develop as a result of that trauma are diverse and personal. However, some general habits that people could develop include suppressing the emotions and experiences that they've had by normalizing and rationalizing the trauma, using avoidance to hide their true emotions and how different situations impact them, being afraid of discussing their trauma due to how others could view them or how it will impact others if the truth is revealed, and using outside elements—such as food, drugs, or alcohol—to engage in unhealthy coping skills.

Identifying your past traumas and recognizing how that trauma guides different parts of your life and actions today is the next step on your path to shifting your mindset and gaining control over your life.

Reflection:

Below are some questions to reflect on. These questions are intended to help you gain a better awareness of the traumas that you may not have paid much attention to and recognize the effects those traumas may have on your actions today.

Who was the authority figure in your house?

In what tone did the authority figure in your life speak? Was it loud, irritated, and/or aggressive? Was it soft and/or peaceful?

How were you disciplined as a child?

How did you respond to discipline?

Are there any moments from your past that make you put up a mental block?

Have you ever shared your experiences with another person? If so, was there something that you didn't feel comfortable sharing? Why did you feel that discomfort? Was it because of the other person, or the memory itself?

As stated above, different people can develop different habits based on the past traumas that they've experienced. Based on the habits listed above and your own understanding of yourself, are there any habits that you think you've latched on to due to your childhood traumas and experiences?

A way to move forward with managing these unwanted habits is to acknowledge the disadvantage they have on you in the present and then to identify the advantages you'll have in life if you were to let go of the habit. After identifying those few habits, create a list of new habits that you can form to replace the old ones. As you practice replacing that habit, be sure to observe how you feel about yourself and the situation, adding this self-awareness to your already established self-care routine.

Journal Your Thoughts & Feelings

Chapter 10

Abandonment

When you left me, my heart sank. When I found me, my smile grew.

This topic hits close to home on so many levels. As I mentioned in the previous chapter, my mother was the sole authority figure in my household growing up, leaving me to take care of my younger siblings. This was because of the tumultuous relationship between my mother and father. My father did not live in the home. However, as a child, he would often try to be an active participant in my life. However, when I was twelve, my father randomly moved out of state. He didn't tell us, and instead we found out by chance. I later learned that he was battling with his own challenges that he'd never discussed with us. But even when he was around, I felt detached from him. He came and went whenever he wanted to, never being there when I needed him. His leaving completed my detachment; yet, his abandonment also impacted the relationships that I would have later in life.

Without my father, I didn't feel protected or secure in my home. As I got older, I became increasingly afraid of the boys and men in my life leaving me. I carried that fear and detachment around with me for years until I realized that him abandoning me was not my fault. I learned to recognize that my father was a human being who was struggling and an individual who did not have the capacity to be a father. I learned to supplement the lessons about men that my father would have given me with books and my own experiences. I learned to create my own sense of protection by, above all, enhancing my spiritual connection with God. I learned everything that I needed and learned also to accept and forgive my father for who he was and is. These steps made looking back on my past abandonment issues unnecessary for the present. All of my needs are met now.

Abandonment is what a person can experience after feeling left out of a significant other's life. If you are consistently abandoned by the same individual or by the same types of figures in your life, it can leave you feeling as if you did something wrong to initiate their lack of involvement in your life. This is what I went through with my own father, telling myself that I must have done something to make him leave, that I wasn't good enough to make him want to stay in my life. This affected my future relationships with men and my own self-esteem.

When a child feels abandoned, it commonly derives from a parent or adult consistently not following through on their promises. For example, many children have had issues with their fathers not living in their household, who would pick them up to spend time with them outside of the home. The father would sometimes show up, and other times he wouldn't. This vicious cycle can cause issues within the child because they do not have an understanding as to why it happens. Kids are very innocent and get excited when you tell them things and, trust me, they always remember! If a child has a good memory, this type of scenario may repeatedly replay in their minds. The child lacks understanding, so the reality of what happened can cause them to grow to learn and accept the disappointment of people not following through on their words. This can also cause the child to blame themselves for their parent's actions, even when they could not have been at fault. Everything that a parent or adult role model teaches a child plays a significant role in how they will view life later on.

As a child, was there someone in your life who often came and went? Do you feel as if many people whom you have loved throughout your lifetime have left you with a broken heart? Do you have an intense fear of new people coming into your life and abandoning you?

If so, you may go through life feeling as if you're unlovable or as if you have to guard your heart to avoid more abandonment. This can cause an energetic blockage in your life, where you attract more individuals who will repeat this behavior.

My experience with abandonment affected me first as a child, and then while in several romantic relationships as an adult. I didn't quite understand that it was a personal issue for me, and I didn't know how I should respond to it. I'd like to say that I was functioning fine during the conflicts that arose from my choice in a partner and my past abandonment issues, but looking back on it now, I was torn and confused.

Your abandonment issues can spill over into friendships and affect how you respond to conflict. Rather than working out your problems with others, you could become more likely to abruptly exit others' lives when things become overwhelming for you. You may let go of attachments quickly while holding on to older, more volatile ones. The older ones may have been formed as a result of a traumatic bond—such as you and the other person relating on past abandonment experiences—which can make it harder for you to release them when they become damaging to your wellbeing.

Everyone's definition of abandonment may look different. This is because of the completely individualized experiences that different individuals have in their life. For example, you may have had a relative leave, but see the situation as beneficial rather than as an abandonment. However, this isn't the case for everyone. As I mentioned above, a result of my abandonment issues was me consistently choosing romantic partners that were prone to abandon me again and again. I became blind to their red flags, too absorbed in my own need to feel wanted than in evaluating whether or not they were a stable person to be with.

Reflection:

There are a few common red flags that can signal whether or not a person will eventually abandon you and that can determine whether or not you suffer from abandonment issues. As yourself these questions:

> Do you fear people leaving your life?

Are you reluctant to let go of unhealthy relationships?

How do you feel when you aren't with your significant other? Do you feel the same amount of self-worth with them as you do when you aren't with them?

Does your significant other ever threaten to leave you?

Does your significant other often cancel or neglect to show up when you two make plans?

Does your significant other ever make promises to you that they never follow through on?

If you answer "yes" to any of these questions, it may be time to analyze the role that person plays in your life and determine whether or not they are a healthy presence for you.

Think back on your own past. Have you ever felt abandoned by another person?

Who abandoned you? Why do you feel they did?

Do you blame yourself for it in any way? If so, why do you take fault in their behavior? Was it your idea for them to abandon you?

How do (did) you respond to feeling abandoned?

Is there something that you often say to yourself about it? If so, what is that?

83

What do you feel that you missed out on due to abandonment? Were you able to obtain whatever you missed out on in other areas of your life or with different people?

Is it possible for you to now provide yourself with what you missed in life? Allow yourself to meditate on creative ways to give whatever you feel you have lost to yourself. For me, this involved engaging with books, with connected more to God, and with developing a deeper relationship with my friends and son. You hold power in your life. Be free from latching onto the behaviors of others. The longer you hold onto hurt, the longer you will suffer. Are you ready to stop suffering?

Journal Your Thoughts & Feelings

Chapter 11

Family Issues

If it's not one thing, it's another. Where do we
go from here?

No matter what type of family you grow up with, many people see their families as important. You gain the most influential experiences in your life from your family. The family is considered out first set of friends and leaders, and many rely on their family for support or to gain knowledge. The amount of time that you spend with your family allows you to absorb behaviors and ways of thinking that can either be beneficial or harmful. In this way, your family can shape the values and beliefs that you hold.

However, as many grow older, some of the traditional family values that they have grown up with begin to change. With this change, some family members become detached from others due to a change in their perspectives.

I've learned that, while family is what you are born into and has the most influence on your life growing up, a family can carry some unhealthy generational ties. This is especially true for my own family;

along with the cycle of abuse and abandonment that I explained in the previous chapters, my family held other harmful generational ties. These include many members having a lack of understanding about themselves and being detached and afraid to embark on their true life purpose. To add, there is a general low motivation for achieving an education and financial independence which has caused many of my family members to have a struggle, rather than a thriving, mindset.

Other unhealthy generational ties can include a history of poor health, financial illiteracy, nonexistent conflict-resolution skills, and limited reflection on life. When you start to shift away from your familial norms, you begin to see these dysfunctions that used to feel normal to you. You may even begin to question yourself, the characteristics of the family that you love, and develop a desire to part from the family. All of these responses are indications that you are on a path toward self-discovery and growth.

Many of the generational issues within families can stem from different challenges, from alcoholism to sexual predators. Many family issues are swept under the rug and not addressed publicly. As a result of this avoidance, blow-ups and fights can occur, causing different family members to play the role of problem-solving within the family. Those who try to mend past family issues with high expectations of family members can often have more stress added to their lives. While you may desire your family to be close-knit, it's too much for one person to do all of the work to bring the family together. Each member has to be responsible for their contribution to the family dynamic.

Are you someone who tries to mediate your family when issues arise? If so, think about how heavy you feel when trying to combat these familial issues; this task ends up taking your focus away from things that you have control over. If you're repeating this cycle of mediation, you will eventually burn yourself out and become resentful toward your family.

I had to deal with a similar situation. After years of trying to mediate the tensions between my family, while also acting as a surrogate mother to my siblings and dealing with my own self-esteem problems, I started to feel as if I was on the end of my rope. As I got older, I accepted the fact that I had to distance myself from my family in order to heal parts of myself so I wouldn't project any of my own challenges onto them. I knew that my family could not help to heal me from something that they hadn't learned to heal themselves from yet. So, I took the initiative and, instead of trying to control the dynamic between my different family members, I controlled myself, stepping away from the situation and focusing on what I could do to help myself and, in turn, help my family.

Sometimes, doing nothing at all is the best thing that you can do to address a situation. Think about it: your emotions are running high, and you may react out of fear, defeat, or desperation. How would that be good for you or your family? Conflict within any relationship is typical; however, how you address it is crucial. You should permit yourself to revisit family matters at a later time if you feel that the situation is out of your control or if your emotions are out of your control.

I've learned to do this through my own family. I have learned to accept my family for who they are, and I engage in family celebrations as often as I can to help keep a healthy connection with them as an adult. However, my relationship with them has changed throughout the years. Rather than focusing on mediating their problems, I have learned to prioritize my own emotions, leaving the situation when I feel that it would be damaging to me. I've learned that the lives of my family members are their own, and I have no control over that.

Reflection:

Think about some of the habits (both beneficial and harmful) that your family has engaged in.

Do you still practice some of those habits now?

What are some of the benefits of those habits? Some of the drawbacks?

Are there any habits or thought patterns that you have learned from your family that you want to change? What are some ways that you can replace those thoughts?

Now, think about the last time you spent with your family. Was there any conflict or tension? How did you react to it?

The next time that you find yourself in a tense familial situation, ask yourself: Do I need to be involved in the situation at this time? What can I do to change this situation?

If you find that you have no control, focus on the aspects that you can control. Do you have control over how family matters or history affect you? If yes, then start there. Allow yourself to feel the emotion in order to recognize that feeling in future situations and know when it is time for you to exit the situation.

If you're particularly overwhelmed, head back to chapter 7 and practice the sense-based grounding exercises to calm your emotions and focus on the things around you that you can control.

Journal Your Thoughts & Feelings

Chapter 12

Unlearning Old Belief Systems & Patterns

You do not have to carry your childhood beliefs into your adult life. Allow yourself to be your own person.

During your adulthood, you may reflect on how you were raised. You may start to see things from a different perspective now that you've had life experiences that have helped you to understand what may not have been clear to you during your childhood. When you take time to look back on life, there may be some things that happened that now cause you pain to think about. There may be harmful actions that you are taking on yourself and others now that you were exposed to as a child. You may have patterns of thinking that constrain you to the life you used to live and that prevent you from growing into the person that you could be.

We are shaped and molded by our experiences. But we can't let this idea keep us in a constant state of blaming our present bad behaviors on our past. As I have explained earlier in this book, because of the interpersonal violence that I witnessed as a child, as an adult, I would often use harmful tactics in relationships, replicating what I thought a functioning relationship looked like. It was only after I reflected on my past and recognized that the actions I was taking were harmful did I break away from that pattern of relational violence.

You may have held onto the excuse that you are just a product of your upbringing and environment as a way to justify your current harmful reality. What is stopping you from reflecting on your actions today and determining whether or not they are beliefs and patterns that you want to continue engaging in? Sometimes, these self-reflections can only happen when we have moved away from the situation that we have based our harmful actions on.

Are you still living in your hometown or near people who have given you harmful childhood experiences? For me, I was only able to reflect on my harmful actions when I moved from my home state. I was also able to outgrow my fear of my family and my complacency in their behaviors. I was able to start challenging myself and step outside of my comfort zone to become the person that I know and love today.

When you move away from where you grew up, you may begin to do as I did: see life through a new set of eyes. Somethings during this phase of your life, you will disconnect from family and friends. This isn't usually intentional; however, this disconnection gives you a reset to life. It allows you to move away from people who have negatively influenced you your entire life and figure things out on your own. But it *is* an uncomfortable transition because it may require you to shed layers of yourself to allow space for new insights and knowledge of your life to grow. When I did my own moving away, I learned that anything was possible. I used to limit myself and was fearful of being assertive to others. I avoided conflict with others in exchange for the internal conflicts that I battled every day. I was afraid of speaking my truth and my opinions about certain topics. But, by moving away, I was able to shed these fears. I learned that my past was only a small portion of my life and that everything in the present and future could be created and designed with healthy ways of thinking in mind.

This new information that you will obtain and experience will eventually direct you toward your life's purpose, where discovering who you can become will be more important than adhering to what your family expects of you. You may get a newfound sense of wholeness when you start to create this new version of yourself.

Moving out of state and traveling also allowed me to see how at peace people can be when they are exposed to more, diverse opportunities and adventures. For me, growing up in a small city, you grow up around the same peers who are all exposed to limited opportunities for career, social, and community involvement. From my travels, I was able to understand why many people in my family felt complacent in their lives and why it was important for me to change my environment and explore alternative ways of living.

Have you ever experienced culture shock? When you move away from the situation that you've lived in your entire life, you may be introduced to different cultural habits that will cause you to alter your perspective on your own culture and beliefs. Sometimes, you can get so disconnected from your familial culture that you start to question whether they were positive cultural habits to have. You question whether you wanted to be invested in that culture in the first place, and what place those beliefs will have in your life in the future. After moving away, I began to spiritually evolve away from the beliefs of my family. This created an initial rift in my family, where my mother had difficulty with my spiritual views. But after I took the time to educate her about my beliefs, she became more open and supportive and grew to understand them.

This questioning of your familial culture can lead you to new insights about your personal beliefs and values. And they can also give you the opportunity to reconnect with your family in the end by sharing with them the new insights that you have gained. This, while initially uncomfortable, will allow your family to learn more about you. This is where you start to become one within yourself and feel more at peace and secure in the knowledge that you have. The shift to getting to this phase is just that: an uncomfortable shift in life. However, it can be very beautiful at the same time. It's the same as any birthing experience; you never know how things are going to go, what bumps you'll have along the road, or how you'll be affected by the challenges. You may take some pauses and even leaps throughout the journey. However, if you allow yourself to embrace the moments you will experience rather than passing them up, you'll have more desirable life outcomes.

Reflection:

Reflect on the following questions:

What are some of your old belief systems?

Where did they derive from?

Do you feel that these beliefs are no longer beneficial to you? If so, when did you begin feeling this way?

Which beliefs do you still keep, and why?

What new belief systems do you have?

How did your family react to your new beliefs?

How did you respond to their reactions?

Does it bother you that they feel this way? If so, please refer back to the self-esteem exercises to allow you to focus on what makes you happy. Sit with that emotion and focus on how you feel about your beliefs. That should always be the action that you take whenever someone criticizes something that you strongly believe in and follow.

Journal Your Thoughts and Feelings

Chapter 13

Wholeness & Intimate Relationships

Intimacy with oneself can bring about more pleasure in an intimate relationship.

When I was young and inexperienced, I made decisions based off of emotions and ignored the logic behind being in a relationship with someone. Rather than choosing a partner based on how we could complement each other, I sought out relationships to make myself feel whole. I was unaware and lacked understanding of how relationships should operate. I lacked self-love and was never taught to uphold specific standards and values. I often ignored my own desires in hopes of feeling complete and was convinced that a relationship was the only way to achieve that sense of completion within myself. Unsurprising, this mindset led to me having a lot of tumultuous intimate relationships.

Have you ever had a desire to be in an intimate relationship because you wanted to feel loved, secure, and happy? You may feel like you are lacking in these emotions and think that, if you were to have someone to love you, then you may feel whole. Some can't love themselves entirely on their own due to their perspective on love. However, love doesn't have one meaning; it can be a multitude of things. They say that you have three "loves" in your life: your first love, where you were young and inexperienced with relationships; the second, a love that causes a massive shift and formation in your character; and the third, well, that is your real love, the love that you connect with after you've transformed and removed unhealthy ways of thinking and habits towards relationships.

They also say that you will not be fully prepared for the first two loves, but with the third one, you'll have enough experience and healing to be presented with the love that will help elevate you further. Does everyone experience this? Well, everyone has a different life path. Some may encounter their true love first, and others may never experience healthy love in their lifetime. Overall, it's up to each person to decide how dedicated they are to healing from past experiences that have broken them and that have warped their ideas of intimacy. Often times, these past experiences are what keep up from finding fulfilling, loving relationships. Brokenness comes unexpectedly, and it can be undeniably painful. Yet, all pain can be transformed into something beautiful, as long as you're willing to understand the purpose and lesson behind it.

Have you ever felt whole in your life? Many will say no.

What does it mean to feel whole to you? For me, feeling whole is being self-sufficient, loving myself, and creating constant peace in my everyday endeavors without the need for others' validation.

It means learning about myself in and out, being satisfied with who I am today, and taking action toward bettering myself daily. Feeling whole to me means making decisions based on how I feel, rather than being unnecessarily influenced by outsiders to act against my instincts.

Some may identify feeling whole as having material items while others look at it as being mentally stable. If you have yet to experience "feeling whole," it is essential to know what this feels like without relying on another person to provide you with wholeness. When you can feel whole on your own, you have the ability to heal yourself throughout the challenges and barriers that come your way. You can overcome the different heartbreaks and rejections that come in life. Many times, when one is feeling less than whole, there has been a sudden change in their lives that has drastically changed their view of themselves or the world around them. Something that you may have leaned on for support, such as a job, a friend, a partner, has changed, and you are left fractured within yourself. These are the times when you need to work on rebuilding yourself without the need of an intimate partner, putting yourself back together piece by piece so that you can be your complete self and better love yourself and your eventual partner when they do come around.

Have you had a desire to feel whole again after a failed relationship? A typical response would be yes, as it is natural for you to want things to be healthy and to make the hurt or sadness that you feel go away. No one wants to be sad on purpose. You can choose to keep living for yourself and finding solace in what you were able to gain from each relationship.

Is it painful for you to think about past relationships? If so, it's time to remove the hurt and break down the pain so that you can eliminate it from your life. This isn't an overnight process; instead, it takes time and a consistent habit of reflecting on yourself, your emotions, and your actions. It will take some time, but you must tackle each relationship separately so that you can finally have your breakthrough.

You have to recognize that you can't just push the past relationship experiences that you've had to the back of your mind. No one truly forgets things. But when you push undesirable memories from past relationships into the back of your mind, you're trying to force your brain to dismiss the memory. Ultimately, what you'll end up doing is suppressing the thoughts and stuffing them down until there is no more room in your brain for your present reality and no more room to build upon yourself. At this point, everything will begin to resurface without your desire at random times, which will greatly disrupt your daily life and keep you in a constant state of reliving those painful relationship memories.

This act of forcing yourself to forget may be the reason that you have unresolved intimate relationship issues. It's easier to blame a person for something and then move on, but how can you move on when you're still holding on to the hurt? You didn't let the pain go with the blame; instead, blaming lets you feel temporary peace. Imagine you taking responsibility for allowing that person to come into your life, and while you were accepting their behaviors and red flags, this heartbreak was in the works. You may have had intuitive thoughts that came to you toward the beginning of the relationship, but you may have been focused on the idea of love and the person's initial presentation, wrapped up to the point that you looked past some significant red flags. Sometimes we don't want to accept this truth when presented with it, that we are partially to blame for the past relationships that we engaged in. It's ok to admit it; we've all been there a time or two before.

How can you be whole when you are still holding on to these past relationship experiences? How can you engage in future, healthy relationships when you still aren't able to feel whole within yourself?

You have control over how you mentally move on from a past relationship. From this, you have control over your ability to make yourself feel whole after a relationship has ended. You can do this by first building intimacy within yourself.

Reflection:

How do you build intimacy with yourself? By removing the intimacy blockages that you have created with others and with yourself based on your past heartbreaks and challenges.

In order to remove your intimacy blockages, you must identify and understand the root cause of their blockage and how it has impacted you. Building confidence in speaking about your blockages with close friends and relatives can also help. You can communicate it routinely to work through the barriers with a supportive person or professional. And finally, allow yourself to be open-minded about exploring new ways of engaging in intimacy and then experiencing it.

Reflect on these questions:

> When you think of a perfect, whole version of yourself, what do you imagine? Do you imagine yourself with a partner? If so, why do you imagine this?

> Think about your past relationships; what was the reason that you chose the partner that you did? Were you seeking the above version of yourself? What is appealing about that person?

> Before your previous relationship, did you consider yourself as feeling whole? How is that different from how you feel now, after the relationship? Is there something that is missing that you had before?

> What does being whole mean to you? Are there any aspects of yourself that you want to build upon or alter that can help you achieve this sense of wholeness?

Journal Your Thoughts & Feelings

Chapter 14

Building Relationships

Support systems change as you age, but you don't have to let that hold you back.

Having a solid support system is one of the most important aspects of my life. Whether it's personal, intimate, or professional, relationships are always evolving. Therefore, the people who you surround yourself with should hold value in your life. My support system is made up of the people that I value in my life. This includes, most importantly, my son, who I value the most. My son is the biggest source of support in my life. I take pride in being a mother, and I feel that my influence over his life has caused me to value our relationship above any other. I also value my siblings as I feel obligated to uphold a supportive and nurturing relationship with them due to being the oldest. While I know that I'm not perfect, I am honored to be able to show them that anything in life is possible.

What type of support system do you have? Is this support system limited? In life, we need to have social interactions that are loving and meaningful; are you open to establishing new relationships to increase your support system.

What does a support system look like?

It can consist of having people who pour knowledge into you, who assist you with resources, who help you look at things from a different perspective, who motivate you to do things that you desire in life, who listen to your concerns, and who offer emotional support. Every person that you have in your system does not have to display every single characteristic; however, it's good to have a collection of individuals that you can go to for different things, especially perspectives. This helps you broaden your analytical skills and helps you to think outside of the box and grow. In order for the support system to be effective, you also should consider your role within the relationships you have. Roles can change over time; however, having a clear understanding of your roles will help you operate in a manner that aligns with your values and beliefs. Effective communication and understanding of your roles concerning others are key. To add, knowing the characteristics of a support system that you value the most will help in your path toward constructing an effective support system. For me, I value the time and effort that's put forth towards maintaining a relationship with me. I enjoy having random conversations and check-ins from my support system.

What are some of the characteristics of your ideal support system?

Throughout your journey, your support system can change and evolve. Meeting new people is a given in life. As you get older, you change your perspective on what needs and desires you have in regard to friendships. You will get to a point where you've outgrown some friends, and that may leave you feeling stuck, battling with yourself on why you are friends with that person and what value they give to your life. I recognized that I had to let go of a relationship when I became overwhelmed with keeping the relationship afloat. I would recognize that nothing was being reciprocated and it would leave me feeling drained and unappreciated.

Have you ever gotten to this point in one of your relationships? If so, it may be time to reconsider whether that relationship is worth holding on to.

On the other hand, if you can have a healthy exchange of information given to and from the other person, then that may be a relationship worth holding on to. If you find value in the relationship, establish what that value is and how you can build on it to continue growing it. Identifying the benefits of the relationship and how they align with your everyday life is crucial. In this way, you will be able to learn more about yourself and your values, and you will ensure that the people in your life are beneficial, rather than harmful, for your growth and journey.

Reflection:

In order to build your support system, it is integral to reflect on your own values, your past relationships, and your current relationships, in order to determine what you need from a support system and the types of people that you want to fill your support system. It's important to release old, toxic relationships and work on healing and gaining an idea of the lessons that you learned from each of those relationships. Then identify what you are passionate about and routinely attend events and social activities in public areas where you can connect with new people. You will be able to naturally navigate toward people who are more like minded and open to building new relationships. My advice is to never look for new situations without closing out the past ones and renewing your mind about specific traits that you need out of a relationship that aligns with your values and belief system.

Reflect on the following questions:

What do your current relationships look like?

What do you gain from these relationships?

What are some things you'd like to change about the relationship?

How have you built relationships in the past?

Who are those 1-2 people you are drawn to the most? What draws you to them? What do you have in common? How are you able to help benefit one another personally?

Journal Your Thoughts & Feelings

Part 3

Taking Control of Your Life

Throughout this journey so far, we have looked at our present lives and the different actions we can take toward our own self-discovery. We have also looked to the past to determine the sources of our conflicts. Now, it is time to use these new insights to learn how to take control of your life and work toward a better, happier version of yourself for your future. This is our final step toward radically shifting your mindset and becoming the you of your dreams.

Chapter 15

Letting Go of Control

The things that hinder you may very well be your tight grasp onto things that are not meant for you to have.

I know it sounds contradictory to start a section on control with a chapter about letting go of it, but bear with me. Control means that you have the ability to make changes to a situation that you are presented with. Oftentimes, we try to control situations through force or persuasion. In this way, we are trying to control situations that are out of our hands, situations that we have no power over. When you respond in these manners, it can lead you to more conflicts; there can be internal conflicts, where you begin to question and despise your own limited nature. But there can also be external conflicts, where your attempts at control come at the cost of another person's agency or your relationship with someone else.

I struggled to let go of control over how people viewed me and the things that they said about me to others. I was the type of person to overly explain myself in the hopes that people would understand me and not think negatively about me. I desired control because I was fearful of rejection and abandonment since those are two things I struggled with from childhood.

I learned that others' opinions of me were out of my control when people would reiterate things about me to myself or others; I'd be in complete disbelief that they felt a certain way about me. They were painting a false picture of who I knew myself to be. Through this, I learned that the only things I could control are my actions, how I treat myself, and how I present myself to others. How others viewed me was up to them; instead of focusing on his, I learned that it was more important for me to focus on how I viewed myself and be happy with me.

You have to be realistic about the control that you have. If there's another person involved, then you have to consider their personality and free will. People desire to have control over things because they feel that they know what's in the best interest of all parties involved. Sometimes our values and beliefs drive this idea; however, it may not be in alignment with others as strongly as we think. As humans, we try to control how other people view us by displaying behaviors that are not authentic. One of the reasons why we do this is to fit in with society or to gain the attention of others who we look up to. Overall, this is an unhealthy way of viewing life, and it can lead to opposite results than what we were anticipating.

Having control over everything isn't possible. Why would you want such a huge responsibility of being in control of everything? Why do you feel like you need to be in control? Everyone has free will, so why would it be important for you to take the free will of others to make them do as you say? Do you become overly upset when other people don't do what you say or what you expect of them? This kind of mindset can trap you in a constant state of feeling upset and angry at others for not listening to your and at yourself for not controlling things better. But, if there's one thing in life that you can control, its yourself and how you respond to things that make you upset, confused, hurt, or sad.

Reflection:

Ask yourself: **What are some things that are within my control?**

Here are a few ideas:

- You control how you respond emotionally to situations.
- You control how you view the world and yourself.
- You control the roles that people play in your life.
- You control the type of job you have.
- You control how often you learn new things.
- You control your toxic behaviors or traits.
- You control your ability to practice self-forgiveness and self-validation.

Now ask yourself: **are you satisfied with these things, and why do you feel that you have no control over them?**

Are your beliefs limited to one or two reasons? Why? How can you look at these things from a different perspective? For example, feeling that you don't have control over your employment or work environment could mean that you lack confidence in your abilities or view yourself as deserving less. The result of your thoughts or beliefs will attract jobs into your life that validate those thoughts that you have.

As a part of the self-care routine that you developed in part one of this book, start listing the different things that you have control over. These can be small, day to day things like what you eat for breakfast, or they can be larger-scale things, such as your future goals and plans. Sometimes during this process, your mind may start to wonder and think about the things that aren't in your control, which can cause you undue stress; that's a perfectly normal reaction. Just ease your mind back to the things in your life that you can control to get away from those thoughts.

Be patient during this process if it's a new transition for you. New skills like this take time to convince yourself that it'll work, so you'll often second guess yourself during the process.

Journal Your Thoughts and Feelings

_____

_____

_____

_____

_____

_____

_____

_____

_____

_____

_____

_____

_____

_____

_____

_____

_____

_____

_____

_____

_____

_____

_____

_____

_____

_____

_____

_____

_____

Chapter 16

Feeling Limited

*The only true limitations in life are the ones that we
create and feed energy into.*

I felt limited while working for my past employer and also trying
to build up my business part-time. I felt that I wouldn't be able to
make as much money being an entrepreneur compared to the salary
I was being paid with the employer. I was afraid to take a leap of
faith until taking the leap was all I could do after dealing with severe
micro-managing and other issues with that employer. It hurt more
to go to work every day than my fear of failure, so eventually, I had
to choose. Since October 2018, I've been a full-time entrepreneur.
I immediately started to make more money than the salary I was
being paid and found myself waking up excited rather than dreading
my work. I overcame my limited feelings, which has led me to live a
more peaceful, enjoyable life today.

Feeling limited in life usually consists of you feeling that you are
lacking in finances, love, opportunities, ideas or resources. These
types of limitations make you feel like you do not have any other

options and that you're stuck where you are in life. Having a limited way of thinking about life can bring about actual blockages and limitations. This has been true in my own life; I used to believe that if others didn't see my value, then I'd have to find a way of proving it to them. However, this limited by the ability to see value in myself. I learned that others' opinions of me did not matter as much as my opinion of myself, the one thing that I have control over. I became confident in the idea that, by seeing value in myself, it would be enough evidence to others of my worth to show confidence in all that I do.

When you have a limited way of thinking about life, you shut out other ways of thinking and risk missing out on alternative opportunities that could come your way. In order to overcome this, you have to be willing to shift your perspective on your own abilities and your life choices so that you do not continue to miss out on your full potential.

Whenever you feel limited, it makes you feel low and rejected by other possibilities. However, it is a choice to feel this way, so it's necessary to identify what control you have over the feeling of being limited. What do you tell yourself about possibilities? Is this something that you frequently consider? Not all options are going to be presented to you in person or within your thoughts during the time of the limited feeling. Instead, opportunities arise when you allow yourself to be open-minded to them coming into your life.

The one thing that you have control over is what you believe in, not what it will look like.

When one is feeling limited, fear can creep in if more rational thinking isn't considered. Many people jump to conclusions without doing their research. A person may have a million-dollar idea, share it with one friend, the friend shuts it down and instantly that person impulsively dismisses the thought. In this way, feeling limited can sometimes be impulsive behavior. It may be your go-to excuse for your life that keeps you in a repeated cycle of self-deprivation. If ideas of your own limitations are something that you truly believe, then other possibilities are thrown out and you won't consider them because you've already told yourself not to. Is feeling limited an impulsive behavior you participate in? If so, why? Where did this derive from? Did this come from your childhood? Take some time to think about this and the origination of feeling limited. If this was a learned behavior, reflect on the earliest age you started to learn it. Allow yourself to be more open to possibilities.

Reflection:

Write a list of areas that you've felt limited in: work, education, relationships, finances, living status, etc. Take your time to complete this list. By acknowledging these things, you can start to transition your thought process on them.

After you've done this, the next step is to take the list and start to rewrite your way of thinking. Let's say you have a thought of "I never have enough money, and I will always be broke, I can't get out of this rut." The fact that you feel strongly about this idea will cause things to never get better. The idea of constant struggle is a limiting belief;

it leaves no room for you to consider other options for how your life will be in the future. So, while you're wallowing in your misery, only you can change this. Society plays a role in your feelings that you may never live the life that you want, but society does not have the power to dictate that for you, wholeheartedly! Instead of using the limiting belief you are used to, you should change the thought to "I have enough money to pay for the things that I need at this time, I will find a way to make more money to pay for the other things I desire, all of my needs will be met. Life will get better."

Journal Your Thoughts and Feelings

Chapter 17

Forgiveness

When you allow yourself to release a negative
attachment, it's like a weight has been taken off of you.

Throughout my life, I've been frustrated with my father's absence. But, as I grew older, I started to realize that he had his own unresolved trauma that limited his ability to parent me. This impacted my intimate relationships because I was searching for unknown traits within men that I was lacking in my father, causing significant chaos in my life. I wrote him a letter stating everything that I desired from him and how difficult dating was without him guiding & teaching me. I let him know that I was releasing all resentment that I had toward him. I kept the letter and never intended on giving it to him. I educated myself on the things that my father wasn't able to teach me by studying my past relationships, reading books, and gaining insight from mentors. After I forgave him, I had a new awareness about him being absent and it no longer hurt to see others have close, healthy relationships with their fathers. I learned to be happy for others and not feel bad for myself. I embraced my awareness and looked at how much I learned about life once I did the work.

Forgiveness enables you to release unnecessary baggage and stress from your life. It does not mean that you accept the situation that happened; however, it does mean that you are no longer allowing that situation to linger through the next phases of your life. Withholding forgiveness often creates a multitude of other problems such as hatred, fear, distrust, or paranoia that you shouldn't have to have. Understanding the lesson behind what occurred is of importance, and the actions you take moving forward can represent forgiveness. Is there anything that you haven't forgiven yourself for? How has it benefited you to hold onto it? It probably hasn't been beneficial once you think about it.

Self-forgiveness is more difficult to overcome than forgiveness toward others. Once you master forgiving yourself, you will then see the value in forgiving others or situations that occurred in your life.

Forgiveness is one of the most difficult things to do for those who have experienced trauma. Too many people think that forgiveness means accepting what has happened to them. Due to this mindset, many feel that forgiveness is too complex, and that's not something that they are willing to do. As ugly as it may look to say that, it's what's necessary to heal and move forward in life. If you hold on to your trauma, you allow aspects of it to control you. Forgiveness is what's missing in your life if you look at people in your life who didn't cause your trauma as enemies, as people who are out to harm you, or as untrustworthy in general. There's a fine line between being aware of people's motives and being fearful of their actions.

Everyone that you encounter may not have your best interest at heart, but you will not truly know until you take the time out to naturally and authentically learn their behaviors. It's ok to think the best of things when you're looking at these types of scenarios. So, what's holding you back from forgiving yourself or someone else?

What's the value of forgiveness? Forgiving yourself means that you can obtain peace in an area of your life that was once filled with sorrow. Forgiving others means that you can release the mental control that they have over you and free up your mind to other things that you enjoy. Imagine replacing many small pieces of your chaos with peace: how does the sound of that make you feel? It may feel impossible at first, but as you chip away at one problem at a time, you will feel lighter.

Why should you forgive? You should forgive because not forgiving means that you're holding on to unhealthy thoughts about a person and life. If the person is no longer in your life, forgive them so that you can make room for another person who is ideal for you in your life. However, you are not obligated to forgive them directly; instead, you can forgive them mentally, which will release the strain that they have over yourself without having to speak with them.

How can you move forward afterward? Think about all the things you gain in life when you forgive. Start focusing on the action that you take so that you can start immediately experiencing those things. Overall, you'll become free from the situation and you will have more control over your future experiences.

129

Exercise:

Allow yourself to make time and create a sacred space within your home. During this time, you should feel relaxed and at peace before doing the exercise. Allow yourself to sit in an upright position, comfortably. Then proceed to visualize your old self during the event that left you in an unforgiven state. If you responded out of character during the event and need to forgive yourself, tell yourself, "I forgive you for doing this. I understand that you weren't aware of what you were doing, but I'm here to guide you to respond the proper way now." As you speak these words, visualize yourself taking your hand and guiding yourself on responding in a better manner. Remember, you now have the knowledge and wisdom to no longer repeat this same pattern, and this is why you need to release the feelings that you have in order to grow in your own life and detached from others' negative influence over you.

If you have a hard time forgiving other people, use this exercise to visualize a response to the person or situation that hurt you. At this time, recall the purpose of forgiving the other person, only concerning what this will provide you with. When you forgive, you take back the power that was once given to the other person.

Journal Your Thoughts and Feelings

_____
_____
_____
_____
_____
_____
_____
_____
_____
_____
_____
_____
_____
_____
_____
_____
_____
_____
_____
_____
_____
_____
_____
_____
_____
_____
_____
_____
_____

Chapter 18

Setting Boundaries

I give myself permission to say no and feel good about it.

Boundaries are non-physical barriers that you set in place to let others know what you will and will not allow in your friendships, work, intimate, and/or familial relationships. It's also a way that you show others how to treat you and an indicator of how you treat yourself. If you practice behaviors such as being forgiving toward others for things that go against your values and beliefs, you may need to work on setting up stronger boundaries.

I used to feel obligated to pick up in areas in which other people were weak and I was strong. However, I started to set my own boundaries when I realized that I was being taken advantage of. People weren't reciprocating my actions in any way. They weren't showing me that they truly appreciated my support, but instead, they'd just automatically feel that they were obligated to receive my help without showing support to me in any way. I was drained from feeling like a superwoman, so I started saying 'no' to others when they demanded my help because I truly didn't have the energy to invest in the things that people were asking of me. I was focused on me for once in my life and by doing so, other people no longer had access to me and the things that I worked so hard for.

Why are setting boundaries in all areas of your life of important? You probably hear from others that you need to set boundaries, but when you do it, you may feel guilty. Feeling guilty is a normal response because you are releasing an unhealthy habit of always saying yes. Your brain doesn't know how to react in a peaceful, satisfying manner when you first start to say no because it's unfamiliar with that kind of response. When I began to set my own boundaries, there was an instant change in my relationships between my family and friends. It's common for others to make a person feel guilty for setting boundaries, but you have to know what's best for you and follow those boundaries because they are direct blueprints to your standards and values in life. At one point, I began to feel guilty about my own actions. But, I had to reason with. I spoke with a friend about it and received the support that I needed. Now, I do not have any regretful feelings about any of the boundaries I've put into place. People treat me better and are more considerate when it comes to asking me for things.

When you begin to feel guilty for setting your own boundaries, reflect on the benefits you'll receive by saying no rather than what the other person is going to feel after you say no. The act of saying no helps to stop an unpleasant behavior from another person. It's you taking control over areas in your life and taking the initiative to make better choices for yourself.

By setting these boundaries, you will gain more control over the different factors that affect your life. It will allow you to feel a sense of comfort when you can inform someone of something that you disagree with or makes you feel uncomfortable, and it will give you a better sense of security to know that you have a complete say in how you spend your time.

What does it look like to set boundaries?

Are you a person that always tells others "yes" when you want to tell them "no"? If so, you may want to consider setting boundaries to ensure that you do not overextend yourself. If you agree to do something that you have no desire to do, then why would you decide to do it? If you have a preference to do something else but you often put things on hold to do something with or for someone else, then what do you think you're you telling yourself? You are unintentionally telling yourself that you do not deserve to do things that are comforting or meaningful to you and that others' needs are more important than your own. Now, why would this be a habit that you have? Where does this thought process come from? Have you always been a giver?

There's nothing wrong with being a giver; however, there does come a time when the giver needs to receive. The giver needs to be re-energized to be able to feel whole and keep on giving to others. If no one is filling you up, then how are you possibly pouring from an empty cup? Are you often frustrated that others do not deliver to you what you give to them? As a human, you naturally have needs that are necessary for you to manage over every aspects of your life. There will have to be some people, situations, or habits that you start saying "no" or "not yet" to for these needs to be met.

Reflection:

Ask yourself the following questions:

- Have there been moments in my life where I should have set a boundary? Were you overextended? Did the people that you were interacting with realize that they were asking too much?
- Are there any people in your life now that you have trouble saying "no" to? Who are these people, and where does your struggle come from?
- Are there any things in your life that you have been putting on hold because of your perceived obligation to others? Why do you think you're putting their needs before your own?

Guilt is one thing that you may feel when it comes to setting a boundary; however, anxiety can form when you draw conclusions on how another person might react to your boundaries. One thing that you should do is allow the other person to respond before jumping to the worst-case scenario assumption; however, you have to give the answer that makes you feel most comfortable.

Let's get real; you may need to sit down with your thoughts and have a rational conversation with yourself to motivate yourself to start initially saying no. You have to mentally coach yourself the same way that you would encourage a young child. You'd more than likely be gentle with a child to not hurt their feelings, so approach yourself in the same manner, and you can walk away with less guilt or sadness.

Journal Your Thoughts and Feelings

Chapter 19

Adjusting to a New Life

*Eliminate the fears, and the mountains that you feel in
yourself will disappear.*

I relocated to two different states in hopes of discovering new parts
of myself. In doing this, I had to leave everything behind and venture
on a fresh start. Throughout these changes, I relied on my faith and
confidence in my ability to make healthy decisions for myself and
my son. I conducted online research about the new areas to learn
about the unfamiliar territory I was moving into and connected
with new people who lived in the areas to ensure that I had a solid
foundation for my new life. My blueprint for adjusting to life changes
is to practice self-care, validate myself, believe in my dreams, create
actionable steps, research, connect with others who have more
experience and can teach me the things that I do not know, and push
through all of my desires no matter how fearful I am.

Change is inevitable; this is the only consistency in our lives.
Whether or not we want change, it *will* happen. Change requires
you to adapt to life in a way that can be uncomfortable. With this
adaption comes changes to other forms of living. It's imperative to

normalize the process of change in one area interfering with other areas of your life.

Now that you've gotten this far in the book, you may have had to make a few changes in your life based on the revelations you've received. The one thing about change is that you can control how you respond to it. You can overcome any obstacle that's thrown your way with sudden or expected changes. One of the healthiest things you can do when responding to change is to be mindful of your feelings and thoughts toward it before you react. Rationalizing how you feel is necessary.

Dealing with significant life changes, such as loss of a job, relationship, or another situation, are everyday situations that are difficult for many individuals to adjust to. If you're a person who doesn't deal well with change, every adjustment can be complicated! Providing clear direction to prepare for that change or take action for change is important. It's crucial to challenge the fear that you have by gathering more accurate information to invalidate the fear. The process in which you build up a fear something can be the same process that you use to show bravery. If it's an initial happy and inviting thought about a situation, why allow fear to creep in? If the second thought becomes uncomfortable, then there should be an understanding of where it came from. Below are some exercises to help eliminate your fear of change.

Exercise 1:

The following questions will be especially helpful for those who are about to undergo some radical change, such as a big move:

What are you looking forward to with this change?

What are you fearful of?

How rational or valid are these fears?

How willing are you to open up to a new way of thinking about this change?

What past concerns do you have that you may be connecting this new change with? Why do you think you are doing this?

What are your expectations for this change?

How can you benefit from the change?

What issue do you have with this change?

In order to begin to get rid of your fear, you should practice a releasing exercise. One releasing exercise that I like to do is journaling. I write down all of the things that I'd like to let go of out of my life; for example, *I am letting go of doubtful thoughts about my goals.* After I complete my list, I do deep breathing and meditation to prepare my mind to study and become steeled against any doubts or fear. I then read the list to myself several times until I feel a sense of a release. I may spend 5-10 minutes repeating the list, then, if I don't feel that I've truly released my fears, I will read the list every day to formulate a healthy release pattern. You should focus on having a fresh start with this change rather than bringing old fears into the present.

Write down your fears. Take time to visualize yourself taking everything that you wrote down and pushing it into water to purify it or dropping it off the cliff of a mountain into nature. Once you're finished with the exercise you can rip up or shred the list that you created.

Exercise 2:

Being Present in The Moment:

Being present requires you to take note of everything around you. What do you see when you look at all areas of your life? What does your support system look like? What resources do you have? How do you feel about the adjustment? How do you want to feel if you don't like how you're feeling? What can you do to make things easier for yourself?

Being able to answer these questions allows you to not worry about what's behind you or what's ahead of you. It simply means to breathe and allows things in your presence to unravel naturally.

Practice this exercise as many times as you can by focusing on the environment around you.

Think about the following questions as you complete the exercise:

What do you see?

What can you touch and feel?

What do you hear?

What can you taste?

What scents are in the air?

Take time and purposely identify these things when going into a new space or needing to ground yourself.

Shawnee Palmer

Journal Your Thoughts and Feelings

144

Chapter 20

Wrap Up

Every ending is another beginning.

Now that you've reached the end of the book, congratulations! You've addressed and overcome many milestones that you may have once felt were impossible to do. This journey is for you alone and no one else. Everyone will benefit from it overall, however, it has to be you who does the work because it is you who will weather the storms and bear the fruits of your labor. Was it easy to get through these topics? No! A healing journey is not meant to be simple. Rather, it's to help you unlearn old, outdated habits, create new, fulfilling habits, and learn more about yourself in the process. It's uncomfortable, it's rigorous, it's tiring, but, most importantly, it's anything that you desire it to be.

Looking back at my life now, the most challenging things that I had to overcome were issues that I had with my parents. There was my father's absence and my mother's expectations. I truly learned how to set standards and value myself along with how to love myself first before seeking it from someone else. The relationship with my mother taught me about the trauma bonds I formed with friends from childhood and how our relationship impacted my ability to choose healthy friendships.

When I look back at it all, I feel that I needed those experiences to truly understand who I am. I was taken through those challenges to see if I was capable of doing what I was called to do on this earth. I do not believe in coincidences; I believe that life has helped shape the better parts of me. Do I honestly believe that I needed those things to happen in order for me to be at peace? No, however, my experiences have been integral to my learning and growing, and I know that there would be no life lessons without any of those experiences.

Looking forward to my future, I feel grateful. I am at peace. I am happy. I am whole. I now have a blueprint with a strong foundation that will carry me into the next phases of my life where I will learn new lessons. I feel that we never stop learning and that learning is a choice. I chose to be a student of life and teach others as I have been taught. I turned my pain into a victory, and freedom is what I shall continue to have.

I hope that, through this book, you have been able to start toward your own transformation, and that it will be an integral part of your own life transformation.

This book can be used as often as you need it for different situations or life phases.

As you go forward with your newfound knowledge and connection to yourself, please keep a few things in mind:

1. Pace yourself as you continue to heal and address new life experiences.

2. Create an ongoing check-in routine for yourself so that you are taking accountability for your ongoing efforts to heal yourself.

3. You are not in this alone. Utilize any resources that you may have as support.

4. You came too far to just give up. You weathered many storms, there's no storm mightier than YOU.

Exercise:

As a final exercise, write down all of the new insights that you have gained from this book and some of the things that you want to continue to work on during your life-changing journey toward self-discovery.

Journal Your Thoughts and Feelings

About the Author

Shawnee Palmer is a Licensed Addiction Counselor and Clinical Social Worker. She received her Master's in Social Work from the University of Denver and is the owner of Alpine's Empowerment Agency, a mental health counseling agency, where she is the primary therapist. She specializes in aiding high-risk youth, adults, older adults ages 55 and over, and families who are caregivers to older adults by providing prevention and intervention services. She also connects youth and adults who are experiencing homelessness with local community resources. Her belief is that all people should be protected, valued, and provided with the necessary support and resources to help navigate them through their lives.

If you are interested in learning more about the services she offers or working with her, please visit the websites below:

www.alpinesempowermentagency.com

www.loveandserenitywellness.com

CPSIA information can be obtained
at www.ICGtesting.com
Printed in the USA
FSHW022034260920